FORGIVE

Seven Steps to Finding Forgiveness and Returning to Love

D1559051

DR. CHARLETTE MANNING

Dedication To Dr. Barbara Lewis King

Forgiveness is the key to healing past hurts, moving you into a promising present and a fabulous future.

For over 30 years of research, study, and just living life, I have come to realize that there are four basic ingredients that govern life. The common denominator in all the religious and spiritual teachings is the four ingredients: forgiveness, faith, gratitude and love.

This book focuses on the power of forgiveness and the importance of using it in your day to day life. A Course in Miracles states, "Forgiveness is the means by which we will remember. Through forgiveness the thinking of the world is reversed. The forgiven world becomes the gate to heaven, because by its mercy we at last forgive ourselves. Holding no one prisoner to guilt, we become free."

I consider myself an expert in this arena not because I have had so much experience but because of the aha moment I had about 20 years ago while studying with Dr. Barbara Lewis King. We have all had people in our lives who have impacted the way we think and what we believe. Dr. Barbara was that for me.

A Course in Miracles, asks us, will you learn your lessons through pleasure or through pain? The answer unfortunately for most of us is, we learn our most profound lessons through pain. Dr. Barbara taught me how to reverse that pain and use it to fuel my most creative thinking and understanding of why these unresolved lessons kept showing up in my life. The question then became am I willing to see this situation differently.

Dr. Barbara said, there is no better lesson forgiveness cannot give. She taught me to be still, be positive, be patient, and most of all be grateful for the lessons in my life, because all lessons come for my greater good, even when it doesn't seem like it at the time.

I was the common denominator in the unresolved forgiveness issues in my life and it was up to me to change the way I see things and then the things I see would change.

There is nothing in our lives that is worth sacrificing or compromising the peace that forgiveness brings. No matter the severity of our hurt, or the reason he or she did what they did - nothing is worth compromising the happiness that forgiveness brings.

It is from that premise I share these lessons with you.

Note: Since this writing Dr. Barbara has transitioned this earth plane. One of the things she shared with us when she left Hillside International Truth Center was , she did not retire, she was being reassigned. So I say she has not expired she has been reassigned an assignment she could not refuse.

She will be missed, but her lessons will live on through us forever.

I dedicate this book to the life and legacy of my Soul Mother – Dr. Barbara Lewis King

TABLE OF CONTENTS

CHAPTER 1

FACE YOUR FEARS

F is about facing your fears. Control is the mechanism you use to create order in your life. However, as you navigate through unforeseen and difficult situations, you may find yourself in new and uncharted territories.

As a man thinketh in his heart, so he is.
~ Prov. 23:7 (KJV)

COVID-19 has created not only a physical pandemic on the planet, but it has also created an emotional pandemic. People everywhere have lost something they value as much as life itself–control! For the first time in history as a global community, we find ourselves completely out of control.

So, how do you control your fears when you are in an uncontrollable situation? Yes, you are being challenged and literally forced to view the world differently. However, there is a rhythm and reason amid uncertainty. So, let's look at what you need to do with the fears you are facing.

First, know that **you** are in control of your fear! You may not be able to control what is happening on the outside, but you can control how you perceive those events! So, how do you do that?

Knowledge and information. Don't listen to the doom and gloom on television; investigate the facts! Unfortunately, we live in a culture where the media glorifies tragedy and calamity; therefore, we have to go deeper into the understanding of what is going on and how it will affect us and those we care about.

I have no objection to watching the news, but watching the news 24/7 can be toxic for your mental health and well-being. We all want to stay up to date on current events, but we need not be terrorized by what's happening in the world minute to minute. The media's goal is to keep us transfixed on the "breaking news" not of the day but of the moment. Enough is enough—too much of anything is not good for you! If you have to have a dose of news, then don't take it with your morning cup of coffee. Instead, give yourself time to appreciate that you woke up, and by God's grace, you are still here. Give yourself permission to be grateful for the day before you bombard yourself with continuing negative news. Trust me, if something drastic or important had happened, you would know about it.

I prefer internet news; I don't like listening to the negative voices on TV. I enjoy reading what I am interested in and I disregard the rest. I normally listen to the news from the BBC, who is not owned by Time Warner. I also receive verified information from the CBC or the WHO, so what I am receiving is credible and not full of fluff or doom and gloom. I believe the media's primary function is to keep you scared and not prepared. That does not minimize the importance of being informed; it just means that you need not watch the same content repeatedly.

Second, identify the fear. Understand and adapt to the fears you face. In other words, don't be scared; be prepared. Whenever you find yourself in a circumstance or situation where you feel fear, identify where that fear is resonating in your body. For example, do you feel your heart racing, your hands shaking, your stomach churning, or do you feel yourself breaking out in a cold sweat? Those are signs of anxiety. Once you can identify and acknowledge what is producing the fear in your mind and body, then you can create a spiritual and physical way to deal with it. Some of your fears may be monumental, and some may be minuscule, but every ounce of fear has a dramatic effect on your body.

Fear produces an emotional signature in the body, and even though you can't see the fear, you can feel it. Fear is also a magnet that draws more fear to it. You know the saying, "misery loves company,"— nobody wants to experience fear all by themselves. So, you share your fears rather than facing them, and the more you share the fear, the more fearful you become. Then you look for ways to soothe the fear and anxiety such as eating or drinking too much. But you can't solve your problems through escape techniques or by using the same mindset that created the problem to begin with.

You may be one of the forty million Americans that have been furloughed from your job, and you don't know when or if you will be called back to work. That fear may be monumental for you, and the energy of that fear is spreading across the world.

I work in the hotel industry, and I have been furloughed from my job for several months now, along with many others. My work associates and I are uncertain when we will return to work. When the pandemic first began, we were all confident that it wouldn't last long; however, as the months progressed, we all wondered when or if the hotel would reopen.

Then the speculation began. The company I work for has a Facebook page that allows employees to check in and share what is happening in their part of the world. Some hotel chains are preparing to reopen and some are not. Some jobs have been abolished and some are still in operation, which leads to more speculation. Some employees are worried that the company will force them out because of their age and tenure. This is unsubstantiated fear. This is fear of the unknown. You can't solve a problem you have no control over, and if you can't change the circumstances, you shouldn't worry about them. *If you pray, don't worry; if you worry, don't pray!* Instead, you need to prepare—prepare for the worst and expect the best. It doesn't matter if you are called back to work. What does matter is how you process the fear of the unknown and move forward.

The acronym for fear is **F**alse **E**vidence **A**ppearing **R**eal, and that means you don't know what you know until you know it. Speculation creates anxiety, especially when your speculations are unjustified and just waiting in the recesses of your mind to manifest. Fear can be made to manifest, as can miracles. Decide if you are going to believe the false evidence or if you are going to focus on the great IAM. False evidence does not come from God; it comes from man, and man propagates the deception of fear like wildfire. My grandma said, "Don't believe everything someone tells you. Find out for yourself—that is what leaders do." She told me you can't chase your destiny if you are running from your fear!

Ask yourself if you will be okay if things don't turn out the way you think they should. Will you be okay if you aren't called back to work right away? And will you be okay if you allow things to unfold in their right and perfect way? Will you be okay?

Don't worry about what you don't know—prepare for what you do know! And what you know is you have a talent and a skill that will be valuable to another company in the event your company does not call you back to work. At this stage of my life, what I know for sure is that worry changes nothing. Preparation changes everything! There is always something better waiting for you.

Think about this for a moment. Was there a time when you complained about how much you hated your job? Be honest. Were you at a point where you thought about quitting because you were fed up with your job and told others that you were going to leave? You may now find yourself in a position where you just might manifest that request. Be careful what you say, and be careful what you think because the universe is always listening, and its job is to answer your request!

Fear is fickle, and its only job is to keep you beholding to it!

Therefore, if you change the way you see the world, the world you see will change. If you don't want COVID, then stop worrying about getting it! Become clear about your goals and the steps you are going to take to achieve them. Fear is man-made, not God made.

You can't change the unknown. What you can do is to elevate the level of your thinking, so you can adapt to whatever may occur. If you receive your old job back, you can be grateful for the opportunity, but if they lay you off, you can be confident you will find another position.

When you find yourself in an unknown place in your life, examine your strengths. If time and money were a not a factor, what would you love to do? Start researching your desires and stop focusing on your fears.

Do you not know that your bodies are temples of the Holy Spirit,
who is in you, whom you have received from God?
You are not your own; you were bought at a price.
Therefore, honor God with your bodies.
~ 1 Cor, 6:19-20 (NIV)

Third, if you are not healthy, get healthy. Do you want control? Control your health—you can absolutely do that. The mind, spirit, and body connection are gifts to you from God!

Your story is a collection of the experiences that have shaped who you are. It's something you carry with you and maybe share with others, but your perception of those experiences plays an important role in how you define your story. Only you can decide if it will become a comedy or a tragedy.

God said, "Fear not, for I AM with you" (Isa. 41:10 NKJV). Do you believe that? I mean, really believe that? The creator of the universe said not to fear, so why would you not believe what He has told you? God can dream a bigger dream for your life than you could ever dream for yourself—why would you not believe that?

Share your story—all of it—the good, the bad, and the ugly. Then rewrite that story with the power and the force of the universe behind you. All the experiences in your life have brought you to this moment in time. It is by God's grace that you are still here, and for that you must be thankful.

Fear of the unknown affects everything known. Your fears impact your health, wealth, and relationships. If you are fearful of something, you need to investigate that fear. Knowledge is power, but fear is not.

You don't have to go toe-to-toe with your fears; understand them and empower yourself to rise above the challenges those fears may produce. Focus on putting yourself in a positive mindset, and don't be scared, but be prepared when those challenges show up.

In the book, *A Course in Miracles,* the "ego" is said to speak first and speak the loudest. Fear comes from the ego and not from God. If you truly believe in God, there is no room for egoic, fearful thinking. Uncertainty pervades our modern culture, and when you are uncertain, the fear kicks in. But remember this, fear is a learned behavior and can be unlearned!

So, align yourself with positive energy and neutralize those negative forces that are keeping you from living the life you desire. Don't be afraid—your fears are not nearly as big as you think!

On the following pages, I want you to write your story from your past, and then rewrite it in your present. If you want to create the future of your dreams, appreciate how far you have come and what you intend to do with your future.

How do you define forgiveness?

_____
_____
_____
_____
_____
_____
_____
_____
_____
_____
_____
_____
_____
_____
_____
_____
_____
_____
_____
_____

Is forgiveness an issue for you? Why?

_____

_____

_____

_____

_____

_____

_____

_____

_____

_____

_____

_____

_____

_____

_____

_____

_____

_____

_____

_____

_____

_____

_____

_____

_____

_____

What is your first memory of someone hurting you?
What happened? When did it happen?
What did you do after it happened?
Did you forgive them or get them back? (Be specific.)

_____

_____

_____

_____

_____

_____

_____

_____

_____

_____

_____

_____

_____

_____

_____

_____

_____

_____

_____

_____

_____

_____

_____

Do you forgive with conditions? If so, what are they and why?

_____

_____

_____

_____

_____

_____

_____

_____

_____

_____

_____

_____

_____

_____

_____

_____

_____

_____

_____

_____

_____

_____

_____

_____

_____

_____

What would it take for you to release this past hurt and let it go?

_____

_____

_____

_____

_____

_____

_____

_____

_____

_____

_____

_____

_____

_____

_____

_____

_____

_____

_____

_____

_____

_____

_____

_____

_____

_____

_____

_____

Are you afraid of someone hurting you again? Why?

_____

_____

_____

_____

_____

_____

_____

_____

_____

_____

_____

_____

_____

_____

_____

_____

_____

_____

_____

_____

_____

_____

_____

_____

_____

_____

_____

Is the fear of letting go keeping you stuck in other relationships? How?

_____

_____

_____

_____

_____

_____

_____

_____

_____

_____

_____

_____

_____

_____

_____

_____

_____

_____

_____

_____

_____

_____

_____

_____

_____

_____

_____

What was the gift (good or bad) given to you from your first hurt? How can you use it to empower you right now?

_____

_____

_____

_____

_____

_____

_____

_____

_____

_____

_____

_____

_____

_____

_____

_____

_____

_____

_____

_____

_____

_____

_____

_____

Write a "I release and let you go" letter to that person who first hurt you.

_____
_____
_____
_____
_____
_____
_____
_____
_____
_____
_____
_____
_____
_____
_____
_____
_____
_____
_____
_____
_____
_____
_____
_____

**NOW BURN IT UP! Watch it turn to ashes
and embrace the fact that you are now FREE!**

CHAPTER 2

ORGANIZE YOUR THINKING

You have begun facing your fears, and you now understand the questions you need to ask yourself when situations arise that cause you to feel fear. Answering these questions will assist you in removing the fear and returning to love. You can do this! Your awareness creates the positive energy that neutralizes the energies that are keeping you stuck. But it requires practice, practice, practice!

Foremost, you will need to go through a rebirth process. This rebirth will transform you from the consciousness of anger and hate to the consciousness of faith and love. You don't have to get even; get focused.

It's time to release those things that happened to you in your past. It's not about forgetting; it's about allowing the past to teach you and move you forward to a better life and a better way of thinking.

Regardless of whether you experienced the traumas of child abuse, sexual abuse, racism, homophobia, or neglect, everything that happened to you has made you the person you are today. You have a choice to either become a victim or a victor!

Don't apply reason to the actions of others because you can't take those experiences personally. What you can do is use those painful experiences as teachable moments for your life. It is easy to become a victim, fall into a pattern of self-pity, and then make excuses for why you have been unsuccessful in the past. Past events were significant when they happened; however, it's time to organize your thinking by using the experiences in your life to catapult you into a positive future.

Don't take the negative actions of others personally or seek revenge for those actions. Instead, ask yourself what you have learned. If nothing else, your experiences have taught you what not to do and how to treat others with compassion. The biblical principle of "reaping what you sow" is true, so don't get caught up in the drama because the only loser in that scenario is you.

None of this truth minimizes the hurt or trauma that you may have experienced, and believe me, I could share stories with you that would curl or straighten your hair! I have decades of experience, and what I have learned is animosity and hate will kill you quicker than cancer. There is power in forgiveness, and when you can understand that, you will have strength beyond all understanding. Jesus said, "Father, forgive them; for they know not what they do,"—not for them but for Him (Luke 23:34 KJV)!

Don't think what happened to you was to punish you or to keep you in the muck and mire of negative thinking. Don't believe it was fate or karma coming back to you because none of that is true; the only one punishing you is you!

You can change it all by reorganizing your thinking.

One of my favorite movie trilogies is *The Matrix*, and I watch these movies at least two or three times a year to get myself back into alignment, especially when it comes to organizing my thinking.

In *The Matrix*, Morpheus tells Neo (Mr. Anderson) that if he takes the red pill, he can never go back to his old way of thinking; therefore, Neo is reborn. In this process of rebirthing, Neo's body has to be transformed to match his new mode of thinking. His body becomes weak, and his muscles atrophy; his body has to be recalibrated to match his new consciousness. Morpheus takes Neo into the "construct" where he loads people's brains with new neural pathways and synapses and those electrical signals he calls "the program." In the construct, Neo experiences unlimited possibilities as Morpheus shows him exactly what he can create and manifest when needed.

Morpheus is a man of faith and he knows Neo is *the One* even though Neo does not. Morpheus takes Neo to the Oracle, a mysterious seer, for further guidance. However, the Oracle confirms Neo's doubts that he is not the One. She only verifies what Neo thinks about himself and doesn't tell him the truth because he is not ready to understand and believe the truth about himself. It is not until Morpheus is in danger of dying that Neo goes from unconscious to conscious believing, and that's where organized thinking takes you. Mr. Anderson becomes Neo!

Nothing is true unless you make it true.

Your past no longer exists, and it can only threaten you when you meditate on it. *A Course in Miracles* states, "Nothing real can be threatened, nothing unreal exists, herein lies the peace of God." The things you give your energy and attention to become your reality. That is your construct, and you can load your program any way you want.

Yes, struggle is a part of life; however, it is only part of it. Transformation is the gift that struggle gives you when you are open to receive it. Your struggles are meant to strengthen you, not destroy you. Your past struggles were the sacrifice you made so you could become the person you are right now. By organizing your thinking and putting those thoughts in their rightful place in history, you build your destiny.

What you think about, you bring about.

As we go through this COVID-19 "crisis," your construct is either scared or prepared. On the one hand, you shouldn't be fearful that you are going to catch it, but on the other hand, you should not put yourself in situations where you become vulnerable to the virus. Prepare yourself by preparing your mind, spirit, and body. If you fear you will catch COVID, and if your unconscious mind is open to receive COVID, you will be more likely to catch the virus.

I don't believe anyone intentionally wants to catch COVID, but I believe that fearful, disorganized thinking will compromise your immune system and make you susceptible to catching it. This virus attacks the vulnerable areas of your body. Having a healthy body may not keep COVID at bay, but a healthy mind will.

Besides all of this, preparing yourself means you believe that you are divinely protected, but you also need to put on that pesky mask!

In *The Matrix,* The Oracle said, "Nosce te ipsum," (know thyself). To be in touch with who you are, your construct must be continually loaded with beneficial and uplifting data that elevates **yourself**. No one can define you when your construct is fully loaded with the data that supports your spiritual growth and development. Then all the past hurts will only empower you to become your greater self.

You may wonder how you can become the person you were created to be while maneuvering through the new normal of COVID-19. This is actually the perfect time if you will change the way you see your life because when you do, the life you see will change.

When Neo comes face-to-face with Smith (Neo's alter ego), Smith says, "I killed you, and now here I am unplugged just like you, and you think you are free, but you are not because without purpose we would not exist!" God created you for a purpose and your job, from the cradle to the grave, is to discover and uncover what that purpose is on earth as it is in heaven.

By organizing your thinking, you put your life into categories. For example, you separate useful things from things that are not useful and beneficial activities from nonbeneficial activities. Categorizing your thinking helps you to move forward and fulfill your purpose. Your past is there to teach you, your future is to inspire you, and your present is the gift of creation given to you. Your purpose connects you to the divine, draws you toward others, and defines who you are. Your purpose will also divide and separate you from those things that no longer serve you.

The question is, are you willing to look at your life and the situations you are facing differently? By organizing your thinking, you will realize who you are and whose you are.

You live in a world of cause and effect—what you put out, you will get back. The universe does not differentiate from the good, the bad, or the ugly; it only gives as it receives. Take your failures and your successes and use them as vehicles in your life. There are no accidents in this creation—everything has a purpose. There are no bad things; there are only teachable moments. There are no mistakes; there are only opportunities for growth on the retake.

Now that you have faced your fears and discovered how your struggles can be turned into triumphs by God's grace, you can begin the process of organization. Organizing your thinking requires focus and precision. You also have to acknowledge when you need divine intervention.

If you see it in your mind, you're going to hold it in your hand.
~ Rhonda Byrne, *The Secret*

Get clear and focused. You can change the timeframe but not the vision. Ask yourself these questions before completing each of the following tasks.

T - is it True?
H - is it Helpful?
I - is it inspiring?
N - is it necessary?
K - is it Kind?

List five people that you most admire (living or dead). What qualities do you admire about them?

_____

_____

_____

_____

_____

_____

_____

_____

_____

_____

_____

_____

_____

_____

_____

_____

_____

_____

_____

_____

_____

_____

_____

_____

What qualities do you admire about yourself?

_____

_____

_____

_____

_____

_____

_____

_____

_____

_____

_____

_____

_____

_____

_____

_____

_____

_____

_____

_____

_____

_____

_____

_____

_____

_____

How have these people influenced your life?

_____

_____

_____

_____

_____

_____

_____

_____

_____

_____

_____

_____

_____

_____

_____

_____

_____

_____

_____

_____

_____

_____

_____

_____

_____

_____

_____

What do you believe is true about yourself? *(Have you allowed others to define you? For example, have you played small because society says, you're too old, you're black, you're a woman, you're too fat, you're a Muslim, you're gay, you're poor?)*

_____

_____

_____

_____

_____

_____

_____

_____

_____

_____

_____

_____

_____

_____

_____

_____

_____

_____

_____

_____

_____

_____

List five of your attributes – *(An attribute is defined as a quality or characteristic in a person.)*

_____

_____

_____

_____

_____

_____

_____

_____

_____

_____

List five challenges you believe are keeping you stuck. Why?

_____

_____

_____

_____

_____

_____

_____

_____

_____

_____

How will you turn your challenges into strengths? Everything that has happened in your life has taught you something. There are lessons to be learned from your past experiences. These experiences were not there to defeat you; they were there to teach you. What is holding you back?

_____

_____

_____

_____

_____

_____

_____

_____

_____

_____

_____

_____

_____

_____

_____

_____

_____

_____

_____

_____

_____

_____

How will you develop your personal spiritual toolkit? There are many ways for you to expand your growth and achieve the dreams you have for yourself. You don't have to reinvent the wheel. There is someone out there doing what you endeavor to do. Their end game may not be the same as yours, but the tools they have used to get started can benefit you. For example, if you want to become a writer, motivational speaker, teacher, health coach, or personal trainer, there are people out there already doing what you want to do, and you can learn from them.

_____

_____

_____

_____

_____

_____

_____

_____

_____

_____

_____

_____

_____

_____

_____

_____

_____

_____

What do you want? (Be specific.)

_____

_____

_____

_____

_____

_____

_____

_____

_____

_____

_____

_____

_____

_____

_____

_____

_____

_____

_____

_____

_____

_____

_____

_____

_____

_____

_____

_____

_____

How will you get what you want? What is your plan of action? Include a timetable for each activity.

_____

_____

_____

_____

_____

_____

_____

_____

_____

_____

_____

_____

_____

_____

_____

_____

_____

_____

_____

_____

_____

_____

_____

_____

_____

Building your own personal spiritual toolkit. There are unlimited tools and resources out there that will support you in achieving your vision. However, you must have a strategic plan of action to accomplish those desires. Building a spiritual toolkit will give you the arsenal you need to keep you focused and on track.

Five books you will add to your library:

_____

_____

_____

_____

_____

_____

_____

_____

Five movies to watch that will reinforce and continue to inspire your vision:

_____

_____

_____

_____

_____

_____

_____

_____

Five motivational talks/CDs you can listen to and learn from:

_____

_____

_____

_____

_____

_____

_____

_____

_____

_____

What spiritual practices will you incorporate in your daily routine?

_____

_____

_____

_____

_____

_____

_____

_____

_____

_____

_____

_____

The best way to achieve your goals is to keep them top of mind, so you're always looking for ways to move yourself closer to them—and a vision board is the perfect tool to help you do that.
~ Jack Canfield

Design an image board with your photo in the center. Add pictures that represent your vision for the next six months. Focus on this board every day.

CHAPTER 3

RELEASE IT AND LET IT GO

I release and I let go.
I let the Spirit run my life and my heart is open wide.
Yes, it's only up to God. No more struggle, no more strife.
With my faith, I see the light.
I am free in the Spirit. Yes, it's only up to God.

What good does it do to hold on to past hurts and animosities? How does it make you feel to have bitterness in your heart? Why is it so important for you to hurt someone who has hurt you? And if you are successful at hurting them back, what have you accomplished, and how does that make you feel?

Release, release, release and let it go, already! Holding on to unresolved issues and past hurts does nothing but weigh us down. Someone or something can trigger feelings of sadness or anger in us. We all have emotional baggage in our lives that keeps us in that space of anger and disconnect fueled by substantiated and unsubstantiated misunderstandings. The only thing these emotions do for us is occupy unnecessary space in our heads.

Don't you have more important things to think about or dream about than how angry and upset you are at someone who probably doesn't care how you feel? The negative thoughts are stuck in your head and thus metastasizing in your body, but the people you're angry with are enjoying their lives.

Don't give negative energy a chance to infiltrate your mind and body; you have more significant things to concentrate on. Nobody has the power or the right to diminish your focus or your dreams. That is why you have to release your anger and emotional upset towards others and let it go! The thing about disagreements is they almost always make you the victim. Each time you tell the story, or you think about it, you embellish the details to your advantage.

I worked for Marianne Williamson for seven years, and she once told me a story about a disagreement she had with a friend of hers. She was angry with her friend for a very long time, and every time she would think of her, she would think about the disagreement and become angry all over again. A while after their argument, Marianne saw her friend in front of a store, and her friend was laughing and joking. Marianne couldn't understand how her friend could enjoy herself so much when she had hurt her feelings and left her anguishing over what had happened. It looked like her friend had moved on from their disagreement and was not holding a grudge. Marianne realized that she was the only one negatively affected by what had happened. She chuckled to herself and decided that since her friend had apparently moved on, it was time for her to do the same!

Holding on to grievances doesn't hurt the other person-—it only hurts you. It's not about making them pay for hurting you; it's about you not giving them the power to do that.

There were two monks walking down the road, and they came to a crossway where they saw a woman dressed in a beautiful kimono. There was muddy water on the road, and the woman was reluctant to cross as she didn't want to muddy her kimono. Without thinking, the monk picked the woman up and carried her across the road. After crossing back, he and the other monk continued on their journey down the road. In silence they walked and walked. After a few miles, the one monk said to the other, "You know, you really shouldn't have picked that woman up and carried her like that." The monk turned to him and smiled, "I put her down many miles ago, but you are still carrying her."

Everyone that comes into your life comes to teach you something about yourself. Some come in for a day, a season, or a lifetime, but until you learn the lesson, they will keep coming.

Releasing is about you and not about anything or anyone else. Is it worth getting upset when something happens that goes against your grain? You can't blame anyone but yourself, so release it and let it go, already!

Because we are in the midst of the COVD-19 pandemic, I have been furloughed from my job since March 21, 2020. We received letters letting us know we probably wouldn't be called back to work until the end of July. We all qualified for unemployment, and the company gave us directions on how to apply and receive compensation while we were furloughed. In early June, several of my co-workers were calling and panicking. They were worried about their unemployment and the possibility of being laid off altogether.

I was talking with one of my close friends from work who was extremely worried, depressed, and concerned for her future. I asked her what she thought she could do about the situation. She said, "I don't know!" Then I asked her why she was worried about something that she didn't know. She was perplexed at my question. I told her my minister had always instructed me—*if you pray, don't worry and if you worry, don't pray.* I then asked her if she was okay at the moment. She said yes! I asked her if her rent was paid, and if she had food to eat today. Yes! All the things she needed, she had right here, right now, so what was there to worry about?

Releasing is easy; holding on is hard.

The Serenity Prayer asks, "God, grant me the serenity to accept the things I cannot change, the courage to change the things I can, and the wisdom to know the difference."

Serenity means being calm, peaceful, and untroubled. The prayer asks God to help you accept the things you cannot change. It doesn't ask you to conform to those things; it suggests you accept them, and by accepting them, you can free yourself from the ties that bind you.

We all have emotional wounds, and my earliest memory is the relationship I had with my father and my mother. My father was not the best father that he could have been to me, and he hurt me in many ways. But every time I think about my father and the fact that my father and my mother gave me life, I am thankful.

My mother conceived me out-of-wedlock back in the days when they were doing back-alley abortions. So, the fact that I am even here is a blessing. My father gave me life even though he did not treat me the way he should have. But his actions don't matter now because every time I have a negative thought about my relationship with my father, I immediately think about a positive memory that we shared.

One of those memories was of going with my father to the public swimming pool when I was a child. I lived during the time of segregation in Alexandria, Virginia, and this was the pool that the black people went to. We were a family of swimmers, so we went to this pool just about every day. My father was an incredible diver, and whenever he came to the pool, people would stand around and watch him dive off of the high diving board.

On this day, my brother and I were at the pool, and my father wanted us to jump off the high diving board. I was petrified and didn't want to do it. My father jumped into the water below the high dive and looked up at me and said, "I will be here to catch you; you can do this. Come on, I'm here, jump!" I was still scared, so he told me he would take me to Burger Chef if I would jump. So, I squatted down and looked into his eyes, measuring the distance between me and his awaiting arms. I jumped and, as promised, he caught me! As I wiped the water away from my face, I could see and feel his arms around me. It was the feeling of genuine love and caring. This is the moment I now choose to remember about my relationship with my father.

We all have to find a balance with our memories, and we can focus on the pain or the pleasure. I have chosen to be grateful for the life my father and mother gave me. What I do with that life is up to me, and I can use the lessons from my parents to move me forward or to hold me back.

We can all view circumstances and situations differently if we choose to. I ask God to grant me the serenity to accept the things I can't change. I don't have to get angry; I have to get focused. Change is easy and holding onto anger and bitterness is hard. Find positive ways to deal with your anger and hurt or they will emotionally cripple you.

Find something or someone that adds positive energy and encouragement to your life. Stay away from negative energy; find the good in all your lessons. Ask God what you are supposed to learn from the situation you are facing. Find that lesson and then let it go. Think about a joyful time with the person who has hurt you. Think about the good this person has brought into your life.

Trust me, this is not airy-fairy stuff; this is hard work! Have the determination to move out of the muck and mire of chaotic thinking. Just know those hurts will keep coming up for you until you learn the lesson and will release them and let them go. Then, and only then, will you be free.

I wrote my father a sixteen-page letter before he died, a letter he never got to read. In that letter, I forgave my father and I forgave myself. My father has been dead for over thirty years, and though

I remember everything we had between us, I have dwelt on the positive memories.

Holding on will never serve or enlighten you. It only hurts and keeps you stuck and out of the flow of what God would have you do. Life is simple—it's our thinking that makes it tough.

Ask yourself if the feeling of animosity is serving you right now. Is the hurt and anger benefiting you in any way? Can you change anything about the circumstance or situation right now? And if you can't, then you need to do the five-finger exercise.

Thumbs up – Everything is A-okay right here, right now!

Index Finger – I'm moving forward in the direction God would have me go.

Middle Finger – I release all anger and upset—release it and flick it away.

Ring Finger – I will engage in something new and exciting today.

Little Finger – I embrace and celebrate the little things that bring joy into my life.

Holding on to anger and grief will not make your situation any better. After facing your fears, organizing your thinking, and expanding your own personal spiritual toolkit, you must release and let go all of your past wounds. You are going to thank those in your life that have hurt you because they have taught you, and you will use those lessons to empower yourself and others.

My father gave me life, and my mother gave birth to me, and for that I have every reason to be eternally grateful to both of them. What I make of this gift they have given to me is up to me; it is not up to them. They owe me nothing, and I owe them everything, for without them I would not be here! So, no matter what slings and arrows of misfortune have befallen your life, today is the day the Lord has made, and you should be rejoicing and glad in it.

Let your past be like the images in your rear-view mirror; objects will appear larger than they are, but let the past teach you. Don't let it smother you. Negativity only weighs **you** down, and you don't need or want that. You want to be fully present as God gives you the direction for your life in peace and serenity. That front windshield shows you the promise ahead of you, and you always want to look forward—it is the most natural thing for you to do. You can't move forward with a troubled mind.

Keep releasing and letting it go until all those memories become possibilities for a fuller and richer life! Let it go!

CHAPTER 4

GRATITUDE IS THE HIGHEST PRAISE

The Lord is my shepherd; I shall not want.
~ Ps. 23:1 (KJV)

Today is the day the Lord has made, and I am grateful and glad to be in it right here, right now. Gratitude given is gratitude received. A grateful heart transcends all understanding. The most beautiful thing about gratitude is gratitude can't be bought; it can only be given.

Gratitude is something you feel and a byproduct of something you have done. When someone pays you a compliment that warms your heart, that is what gratitude feels like. When someone gives you a gift that is unexpected and you are overwhelmed with joy, that is what gratitude feels like.

What are you grateful for? Can you name five things that money can't buy that fill your heart with gratitude?

1. _____

2. _____

3. _____

4. _____

5. _____

BODY

*Then the LORD God formed a man from the dust of the ground
and breathed into his nostrils the breath of life, and the man
became a living being.*
~ Gen. 2:7 (NIV)

Therefore, you are the person who God made manifest by the power of His breathing you into being. You are the IAM that God created. You are that! What more could you possibly be grateful for?

IAM grateful that I woke up this morning because thousands of people didn't. IAM grateful for this breath of life, the inhaling and exhaling with no help from me. IAM grateful that I can sit up and throw my legs across the bed and stand up on my own volition. IAM grateful for my eyes to see, my ears to hear, my nose to smell, my tongue to taste, and IAM most grateful that I have a clear mind to think and honor the Lord God who watched over me through the night. I can rejoice that my heart continued to beat, and my other organs continued to function throughout the night, all without my assistance. God blew the breath into me. Now tell me that is not something to be full of gratitude for!

*Be grateful for who you are and what you do, and you can become
anything your heart desires.*

I've walked at least two miles almost every day for the last eleven years. Think about that for a moment. That's marginal considering there are millions of runners who do five to ten times that amount almost every single day.

I've walked fourteen miles a week—that's 700 plus miles a year times eleven years—that's over 8,000 miles in eleven years. This total doesn't include completing normal tasks; I'm talking about intentional walking.

My feet, legs, hips, thighs, abdomen, heart, lungs, and all of my other organs have worked in concert for me to complete this task. My body has done this for me for over sixty-nine years. Now tell me that isn't something to be grateful for!

How do you thank your body?

_____

_____

_____

_____

_____

_____

_____

_____

_____

_____

_____

_____

MIND

I am grateful for all the many blessings I am about to receive today, tomorrow, and in the days to come. I look forward to what God has in store for me. I expect a miracle to happen in my life every day. I don't ask God for anything because He knows the desires of my heart; I just thank Him in advance for all of my blessings.

There is a gratitude language you should learn to speak that will ensure that God's blessings continue to flow through you each moment of every day. There are two words that will assist you in fulfilling the desires of your heart. They are, "IAM!"

When Moses spoke to the burning bush, he asked God who he should tell his followers sent him. God said, tell them "IAM has sent me to you" (Exod. 3:14 NIV). As you can see, I don't separate the letters—I make IAM one word (GOD).

Always follow IAM with positive words, statements, and declarations. For example, don't ever say "I am broke," say "IAM open to receive all the good God has for me today." After thanking God first thing in the morning, I ask God for direction for my day. By doing that, I am asking God for His blessing on my day, and God will give me all the time, talent, and treasure to fulfill His mission for me on earth as it is in heaven. Jesus said that in His Father's house there are many mansions. God isn't cheap, and He isn't broke—so neither are you! You don't know where your gifts are coming from, so don't play God cheap by worrying about the how. Just know that He will provide you with the riches of your heart.

What are your IAM statements?

_____

_____

_____

_____

_____

_____

_____

_____

_____

_____

_____

_____

_____

_____

_____

_____

_____

_____

_____

_____

_____

_____

_____

_____

_____

_____

SPIRIT

Meditate and pray. Affirm to God that every day in every way you are better and better. Every day in every way you are trusting in the power and the presence of the Holy Spirit that dwells within you.

There is nothing to fear when you have gratitude in your heart. When you pray and trust, you never need to worry. Just take your prayers to the altar and leave them there. Take the time several times a day to just look to the heavens and say *thank you*. In the book, *The Artist's Way*, Julia Cameron instructs her readers to say thank you three times every day because the energy of three sets the intention to the universe.

For example, "Thank you, thank you, thank you, GOD for ALL the money I have right here and right now. Thank you, thank you, thank you, GOD for ALL the money IAM about to receive today, tomorrow, and in the days to come."

If you are not in your best health, say, "Thank you, thank you, thank you, GOD for my GOOD health. Thank you, thank you, thank you for allowing me to not only get up but also to stand up on my own volition." It is by GOD'S grace that we can walk, talk, stand, sing, run, jump, or just raise our arms above our heads. These are all gifts to this body given to us by GOD.

When you know better, you do better, and it costs you nothing to be grateful. So, say it loudly and say it proudly, "IAM grateful for all the gifts I have received today, and I enter this day only to serve in the GLORY of GOD! Thank you, thank you, thank you in the name of the Most High...AMEN."

Give, and it will be given to you. A good measure, pressed down, shaken together and running over, will be poured into your lap. For with the measure you use, it will be measured to you.
~ Luke 6:38 (NIV)

How will you thank God in advance for your blessings?

_____

_____

_____

_____

_____

_____

_____

_____

_____

_____

_____

_____

_____

_____

_____

_____

_____

_____

_____

CHAPTER 5

INTUITION — TAPPING INTO YOUR INTUITION THROUGH THE POWER OF MEDITATION

Your visions will become clear only when
you can look into your own heart.
Who looks outside, dreams; who looks inside, awakes.
~ C.G. Jung

The word intuition comes from the root word "in-tuit" which means "to know, sense, or understand." Intuition is not selective—everyone has it! However, it becomes difficult for your intuition to speak to you if your mind is in the past or the future.

The question becomes, how do you speak to yourself? You probably wouldn't allow anyone to say the things about you that you say to yourself. You are your own biggest critic. You say things like, "I am ugly, I am fat, I am old, I don't have enough, I am stupid," and "Why do I keep doing things like this?" Sound familiar? Remember, the Holy Spirit is always listening and answering your prayers; therefore, you must always be mindful of what you say and how you say it.

Your intuition works in concert with the Holy Spirit by sending you the answers to the questions you pose to it. Choose wisely the dialogue you have with yourself—your life and well-being depend on it.

You have the power to develop your intuition and become more in tuned to it when you understand what it is and how it works. Intuition is a conscious consciousness, an awareness or inner knowing expressed through your outer being. When you listen to and heed the instructions of your intuition, it will lead, guide, and direct your path to unlimited possibilities.

Intuition serves as the internal red flag God gives each of us to discern if something is or isn't right. It is that funny feeling we may feel in the pit of our stomachs screaming at us to STOP! Yet, most of us fail to listen and answer its call.

Your intuition works best when you are in a present state of mind. Your past hurts are usually what you focus on because of the fear of repeating those mistakes. However, it is the now moment that will define your future—the gift intuition gives you is its present attention.

Don't feel bad about not listening to your intuition—all of us have done it. In fact, most of us neglect this inner knowing more than we listen to it. The beauty of learning to listen to your intuition or follow your instincts is learning the power of meditation. Meditation is GOD talking to you, just as prayer is you talking to GOD.

Meditation is the one discipline most people will avoid like the plague, but when you learn to take the time to be still and turn your thoughts inward, you will be awakened to the universal source that dwells within us all.

Before you decide about anything, sit down in a peaceful space, close your eyes, tune out all the distractions of the day, and ask the Lord God of your being what you should do. The more you learn to turn inward, the more you will recognize and understand the power of your intuition.

> *Don't let the noise of others' opinions*
> *drown out your own inner voice.*
> ~ Steve Jobs

You will always make mistakes and that's okay; however, when you practice tapping into your inner voice, those mistakes will be the life lessons that take you to the dreams and visions you have for your life.

Take risks! That is really what life is about. You must pursue your own vision and pursue it with passion and determination. No one can live your life for you—only you can do that. You are the one who will create, develop, and determine what the guidelines for your life will be. Trust your instincts. Accept nothing but the best; don't be afraid to fail. Look for and listen to that inner voice. It is the voice of the Holy Spirit, and it will never lie or deceive you.

Don't allow your dreams and your visions to slip between your fingers by listening to those who don't have a clue about who you are and whose you are.

Sometimes, good things come to us quietly, although nothing comes complete. It is what you make of whatever encounter you may face that will determine the outcome. As Sirius Black said to Harry Potter, "Sometimes bad things happen to good people; it's what you do with those bad things that will make you great."

What you choose to see, what you choose to save, and what you choose to remember is up to you—all the answers reside within you. Like the good witch said to Dorothy in *The Wizard of Oz* about going home, "You had the power all along, my dear."

As you grow, learn, and become more masterful in your meditations, you will notice that your intuitive powers will continue to grow and expand. Not one decision in our lives has to be made in an instant, yet we often make some of the most critical decisions without thinking or asking God for help. Ask God first, "What should I do?" Then pause and wait for His answer. If the answer that comes to you is rooted in a past hurt, it is not God. Follow your inner voice and pay attention. God will give you the answer. Then, and only then, should you act!

Still your mind to neutralize the thoughts that bombard you consistently. Remember, your ego is the first and loudest voice you hear. Therefore, the Holy Spirit can't get through to you and sharpen your intuition when you are listening to all the noise of negativity.

Intuitive thinking takes practice. It is like building your muscles; the more you work at it, the better and stronger you will get. You use weights to build muscles; you use meditation to build intuition.

Here are nine steps to assist you in becoming more proficient in building your intuitive muscles.

1) Remove mental clutter - clear mind, clear vessel.

What you think about is what you bring about. Learning to declutter your mind will teach you how to control your thoughts. However, to control your thoughts, be willing to discard the things that no longer serve you. It's true that everything you have done and everything you have learned has brought you to this point in your life and has made you who you are, but there comes a time when you have to let the past go!

Your past experiences may have been significant at the time. Yet, those incidents may no longer be helpful or essential to your current spiritual growth and development. All the judgments, jealousy, envy, and revenge were/are deterrents keeping you from your greater good.

Your past is there to teach you, not enslave or control you. All the past pain and suffering should be the catalyst to bring you to a more organized and promising future.

External clutter is internal clutter on display.

Finding forgiveness and returning to love begins with releasing and letting go of your past. When you change the way you see your life, the life you see will change. Prayer and meditation establish clarity of thought; however, you have to get rid of the negative clutter in your head and open your mind to connect with your inner voice.

What past thoughts are holding you back?

_____

_____

_____

_____

_____

_____

_____

_____

_____

_____

_____

_____

_____

_____

_____

_____

_____

_____

_____

_____

_____

How could releasing the pain of your past change your present?

_____

_____

_____

_____

_____

_____

_____

_____

_____

_____

_____

_____

_____

_____

_____

_____

_____

_____

_____

_____

_____

_____

_____

_____

_____

2) Meditate - tuning in, tapping in, and turning on your higher self.

The mind and the brain are not the same. The **mind** is the creator of thought, and the **brain** is the receiver of thought. Like a radio, the station is the mind, and the transmitter is the brain. Meditation is the tuner which allows you to turn up your frequency and raise your vibration.

The brain is an organ; the mind isn't. The brain is the physical place where the mind resides. The mind is the manifestation of thought, perception, emotion, determination, memory, and imagination that takes place within the brain. The mind is often used to refer specifically to the thought processes of reason.

Meditation can help you eliminate negative thoughts, worries, and anxiety—all factors that can prevent you from feeling happy. The practice of regular meditation has been proven to minimize the symptoms of stress and anxiety.

Meditation is the convergence of mind and brain where harmony and balance are of one accord. Time does not exist in meditation; there is only presence of mind. It doesn't matter what is going on in the outside world; the only thing that matters is stillness and peace. This is where you give birth to your creativity. You can create anything—first from your mind (inside) and then to your body (outside).

The same thing applies to a belief verses the truth. Beliefs come from the brain, but the truth comes from the mind. You may believe you are unworthy, but the truth is you are unlimited. You can always change a belief, but the truth remains steadfast. Jesus says that we can do "greater works than these" (John 14:12 KJV), and "all things in Christ who strengthens" us (Phil. 4:13 NKJV). The only thing that keeps you from that truth is the belief that you don't possess the power and presence to embrace it.

There are many forms of meditation, and how much and how long you meditate depends on the results you wish to achieve. *A Course in Miracles* says, "If you give the Holy Spirit five minutes each morning, He will be in charge of your thoughts all day." You might not be giving the Holy Spirit those five minutes because you don't believe it would make a difference.

If you are new to meditation and you need some guidance, there are many ways for you to begin. I always suggest you begin at the beginning. Just sit! Psalm 46:10 (KJV) says, "Be still and know IAM God." Be still. Yes, the chatter will come, your back will ache, your nose will twitch, and everything that could disturb your peace will come up but be still, anyway. Music is wonderful, but in the beginning, it can be a bit of a distraction. Learn how to take charge of what you are thinking, and when the chatter starts, gently guide yourself back to your center. Your center is the Heart Chakra (which we will talk more about in the chapter on *Energy*) I believe the soul resides in the heart area. Some say it is the energy that makes the heart beat. When you get out of your head and drop down into your heart space, you can feel the rhythm of your divinity. I believe you need to feel that rhythm because it's who you are, and that is where you will learn the inner voice and inner peace of God.

God doesn't talk to you in words; God connects with you through the rhythm of your heart, and your rhythm is unlike any other. It is the personal relationship you have with your source, and you need to know that voice and recognize it on a deep, divine level.

There are other methods of meditation that you may wish to explore, like guided meditations, mindful meditations, and mantras. There are plenty to choose from; however, I believe being still in the silence is golden.

Prayer is your communication with God; meditation is God's communication with you. You don't have to beg God to make things better for your life. All you have to do is sit in His presence and ask, and it will be given to you.

Set your alarm for five minutes - close your eyes and just be.

What thoughts came up for you during this five-minute meditation? Were you distracted? Did you lose your focus? How were you able to bring your attention back to your center?

_____

_____

_____

_____

_____

_____

_____

_____

3) Spend time in nature -
ebb and flow and your intuition will grow.

Nature heals and promotes balance.

Nature will teach you different things depending on your goals. It can teach you how to think more clearly and scientifically, enhance your sense of spiritual connection, or even achieve personal success. It all starts with having an attitude that aligns with your own personal interests.

There are three things I do upon waking. I give thanks for waking up, I ask God what He would have me do, and then I go for a walk. I love starting my day in nature! I love watching the birds, bees, flowers, and trees growing without interruption or destruction. No matter what is going on, nature continues to move and grow. I've often wondered where a bird goes during a thunderstorm. There is a rhythm in nature that is natural. It ebbs and flows; it doesn't resist life.

Nature adapts; humans react!

Even amid this COVID pandemic, nature continues. There is a tree with a bird's nest in my yard, and I have watched as the nest was under construction. The birds went about preparing the space for the mama bird to lay her eggs. There was no debating about how big the nest should be or if they have a one or two-car garage. They just went about preparing for the arrival of new life. After the birth of the birds, the mama bird kept them warm, protected them from the elements, fed them, and then pushed them out of the nest when it was time for them to fly. What an outstanding example of how we should approach life.

No muss, no fuss. Wouldn't it be great to have a life like that? Your dreams will make room for you, and through your meditation, God will answer your request by providing you with the time, the talent, and the treasure to fulfill His tasks for you. But you have to ask God to receive the benefits of His wisdom, and you have to be willing to fly, even in the midst of your fear.

What has nature taught you about the natural order of things?

_____
_____
_____
_____
_____
_____
_____
_____
_____
_____
_____
_____
_____
_____
_____
_____

4) Affirm - boost your intuition with affirmation.

I love affirmations, especially when I am doing battle with my ego. Affirmations help purify your thoughts and quiet the egoic dysfunctional mind, which is constantly playing tricks on you. Your ego never wants to relinquish control over your thinking. As long as it can keep you rooted in the pain of your past or the fear of your future, it has control over you. Affirmations get you out of past/future thinking because they are expressed in the present.

I create my own affirmations depending on what I am or want to do. For example, "IAM a rock on which my dreams are built. IAM the best creation God ever made. IAM inspiration manifest in flesh," and my favorite is, "Oh yeah, oh yeah, IAM!"

Create five affirmations to boost your intuition.

_____

_____

_____

_____

_____

_____

_____

_____

_____

_____

_____

_____

5) Be compassionate toward your body.

*Developing intuition for your body begins
when you hear your body's messages.
Your body can help you understand your inner condition.*

Be gracious to your body; do the things that make it feel healthy. Dr. Oz coauthored a book called *You On a Diet.* This insightful book provides you with the best four steps to optimal health, and I have used this formula for years. Eat right, get plenty of rest, exercise, and reduce stress.

The Spirit of God needs a pure channel to transmit His messages to you. The better you treat your body, the clearer the message.

Being grounded in your body allows you to operate from a place of clear intuition and personal power.

What are five ways you can honor your body?

_____

_____

_____

_____

_____

_____

_____

_____

_____

6) Let go - right here, right now.

If you can't change it, learn from it and let it go. Letting go doesn't mean you forget about what happened; it means you put what happened in perspective and learn an important lesson from it. My father was not a great father to me, but he was the father who gave me life. I let go of the hurt I felt as a child, and I forgave him because I believe he did the best he could with what he knew. How about you?

Who are you willing to forgive, and why?

_____
_____
_____
_____
_____
_____
_____
_____
_____
_____
_____
_____
_____
_____
_____
_____

7) Practice - practice makes perfect.

I have been asked the following question many times and my answer is always the same. *If you could have a conversation with anyone, living or dead, who would it be?* My answer—I will always choose to talk to God! I have some of the most amazing conversations with God, and the more conversations I have with Him, the clearer I recognize His voice. I practice being intuitive, and the more I practice, the better I get at it. I've learned when God says to let something go, I let it go. The God I talk to doesn't need long drawn-out conversations; He says, "Go," and I go, and He says, "Let go," and I let go!

What would you say in your conversation with God?

_____

_____

_____

_____

_____

_____

_____

_____

_____

_____

_____

_____

_____

Who else would you talk to and what would you say?

_____

_____

_____

_____

_____

_____

_____

_____

_____

_____

_____

_____

_____

_____

_____

_____

_____

_____

_____

_____

_____

_____

_____

_____

_____

_____

_____

_____

8) Emphasize the positive.

*Stop being afraid of what could go wrong
and start being positive about what will go right!*

Studies have shown an indisputable link between having a positive outlook and health benefits like lower blood pressure, less heart disease, better weight control, and healthier blood sugar levels. Even when faced with an incurable illness, positive feelings and thoughts can improve one's quality of life.

What happens in the brain influences what happens in the body, and when the body is healthy and happy, your life is healthier and happier.

List five songs that make you feel fantastic inside.

_____

_____

_____

_____

_____

_____

_____

_____

_____

_____

_____

_____

Pick five dances (like the electric slide or cupid shuffle) that move positive energy through your body.

_____

_____

_____

_____

_____

_____

_____

_____

_____

_____

_____

_____

_____

_____

_____

_____

_____

_____

_____

_____

_____

_____

_____

_____

Commit to doing one dance three consecutive times each day. (That is fifteen minutes of positive exercise.)

Love without condition. Talk without bad intention.
Give without any reason.
And most of all, care for people without any exception.
~ Anonymous

Kindness is intuitive—it's over thinking that leads to selfish
behavior. Study after study has concluded that selflessness is
intuitive, and that when people are pressed to make snap-
judgement decisions, they typically choose to be generous instead
of selfish. Over thinking, on the other hand, is what tends to lead
to egocentric behavior.
~ The Cut

9) Understand selflessness.

Selflessness is the mastery of abundance. The Bible instructs us that the way we give is the way we will receive. By serving others and being selfless in our giving, we open ourselves up to receive the riches of God's kingdom.

The universe is never in short supply, and the emptier your cup is, the more the Holy Spirit will fill it up. Morgan Freeman, who plays God in the movie *Evan Almighty*, tells Evan he can change the world through A-R-K (one Act of Random Kindness at a time). The reward for selflessness is a full and abundant life.

Being filled with gratitude enhances your intuition because when you have a grateful heart, you do things with the intention of serving others and sharing your gifts with the world. Your inner voice will guide and direct your path along the intention.

How can you be of service?

_____

_____

_____

_____

_____

_____

_____

_____

_____

_____

_____

_____

_____

_____

_____

_____

_____

_____

_____

_____

_____

_____

_____

_____

_____

_____

_____

CHAPTER 6

VALUE THE LITTLE THINGS IN LIFE

No one can place value on your life; only YOU can do that!

Value the things that go right in your life, but also value the things that don't go right. Give yourself the opportunity to learn from those lessons, even though they may sting a bit.

Life is full of twists and turns that get you off track. We all experience these detours—nobody is exempt. Realize that failures are opportunities for you to grow and to learn how to avoid making the same mistakes again.

I have had more careers than one could imagine. I have certificates and degrees in areas I don't intend on pursuing as careers. For example, I took a certification program in broadcasting, thinking I would like to be a news reporter or do voice overs. I did not establish a career in broadcasting, but I learned how to speak, articulate, and how to communicate in front of a camera or large audience. I never became a broadcaster, but I learned how to write copy, dress for success, and command attention from an audience. So, I received great value out of taking that course.

I went to hair styling school and learned how to do all kinds of hair and nails. It was not a career move, but it was an opportunity for me to become certified, and it provided me a way to have an income in good times or bad. It was of value to me because I had something to fall back on if I needed to earn a living.

Value the ability to come home to a house that provides you with peace; value the gifts that are given to you; and value the things you give to others.

I read this list some time ago from Project Life Mastery[1] that explains how appreciating the little things in life will give you a greater appreciation for the bigger things.

Here are seven ways that you can value the little things in life.

1) Slow down.

Life moves so fast that it can feel as if we are on autopilot.

Journal. Share your feelings with yourself. I have this activity that I do every day. It is called **"750 words,"** and I use this activity to slow down and appreciate the things that are happening around me.

Observe. I go outside on my front porch and just breathe in and let my lungs absorb the fresh air. I look around my neighborhood, and I just take it all in—the trees, the birds, the flowers, the cars going up and down the street; the people walking and jogging, and those going about their daily chores. All those things provide me with a scenic view of evolution and the continuation of life.

---

[1] https://projectlifemastery.com/the-little-things-in-life/

Embrace. Appreciate what you have right here, right now. You may not have all you want, but by God's grace, you have everything you need in this moment. You may not have as much as some, but you have much more than many. Appreciate that!

2) Help others.

Do for others as you would want them to do for you. Donate your talents to your church or social organization. Do something selfless without needing to be rewarded with money or fame—just do it because it's the right thing to do.

3) Value the things you do to help others.

Be a person who is willing to step up and serve others. Helping others doesn't have to involve monetary giving; you can give a hug, a smile, or a pat on the back for a job well done. Share your joy and help others feel peace and joy in their lives.

4) Adopt an attitude of gratitude.

Be grateful for everything in your life. If you woke up this morning, you can make a difference in the lives of others today.

5) Live in the present.

Yesterday is a cancelled check—you can't live it over again, so learn from it. If you made a mistake, then own it, and try not to make the same mistake twice.

6) Smile more.

Smiling is great body therapy. Your body appreciates joy—it produces protein in the body, and disease can't grow in a protein-enriched body.

7) Stop comparing yourself to others.

Unfortunately, in the era of social media, we all compare ourselves to others way too often. Be authentic and only use the success of others as a guide. Be the best "you" you can be.

What do you *value* most in your life?

_____

_____

_____

_____

_____

_____

_____

_____

_____

_____

_____

_____

_____

_____

_____

Are your past *values* in need of an upgrade? If so, why and how? For example, when I was a little girl, my grandmother taught me that "good girls" always wore nylons, (panty house) and "hussies" went barelegged. We know that value has changed dramatically in our present culture. So, what value did you hold in the past you are now willing to change or upgrade?

_____

_____

_____

_____

_____

_____

_____

_____

_____

_____

_____

_____

_____

_____

_____

_____

_____

_____

_____

_____

_____

Chapter 7

Energy is the Source of Life

Instead of worrying about what you cannot control,
shift your energy to what you can create.
~ Roy Bennett

I've saved the best for last. Energy is difficult to explain because it is sensory, and most of you only believe what you can see. Energy is all around you—it's in you, moves through you, and manifests itself to the world as you. You are energy!

You may wonder what energy has to do with forgiveness, and I submit it has everything to do with forgiveness.

Love is more powerful than hate.

David R. Hawkins, author of *Power vs. Force*, writes, "Love is more powerful than hatred; truth sets us free; forgiveness liberates both sides; unconditional love heals; courage empowers; and the essence of Divinity/Reality is peace." Therefore, it is always to your advantage to forgive; it releases the negative energy that keeps you distracted.

Negative energy is dense and uncreative; its primary duty is to keep you stuck in the pain and the fear of your future. However, once you learn how to raise your own energetic frequency, you will understand that your past is a spiritual tool for your guidance and evolution.

We will explore how these energetic frequencies should be used to keep you in the mode of creativity.

There are four types of energy the body produces. In the body, **thermal energy** helps us to maintain a constant body temperature; **mechanical energy** helps us to move; **electrical energy** sends nerve impulses and fires signals to and from our brains; and **chemical energy** is stored in foods we eat. Then there is the "auric field" which is the energy that holds all the other energies in the body together.

This is science and not some *pie in the sky, airy-fairy* kind of mystical mumbo jumbo—this is the real deal—and that is why it is important for you to personalize your learning by investigating these truths for yourself.

The best definition and explanation of the human auric field that I have found is from *Cosmic Magazine*. It combines both eastern and western science.

"The human body is similarly comprised of biological circuits that carry electric current throughout the complex wiring systems of our organism. These electric currents are generated on multiple layers and result in the formation of an electromagnetic field around our physical body, something historically referred to as an aura. Scientific research and techniques like electro-photography have observed that all matter in existence radiates an electromagnetic (auric) field. Scientists have been investigating—and substantiating—the existence of the aura, the human energy field that surrounds our entire body, for over a hundred years, adding to the knowledge our ancestors already possessed. This field consists of multiple bands of energy called auric layers or auric fields, that encompass the subtle body, connecting us to the outside world."

The aura has been known by many names in many cultures. The Kabbalists called it an "astral light." Christian artists depicted Jesus and other figures as surrounded by "coronas of light."

You have astral light that surrounds your body, and the intensity of your light depends on how you work with these energy centers. The higher the vibration, the purer the vessel, and the denser the vibration, the more compromised the vessel. In other words, you have the ability to manipulate your own vibration. This is most popularly known as *The Law of Attraction.*

Faith is the energy of God in your spirit!

You can have two identical situations with the same types of individuals diagnosed with the same disease. Each is treated in the same way with the same medications and may or may not have the same result to their condition. Some may refer to this as the placebo effect—the level of your belief system (faith) will influence everything you do. Faith is the energy of God in your spirit!

Faith is a healer, period! Faith, however, is not for the weary. It takes unwavering belief and constant focus. You literally have to take your prayers to the altar and leave them there. Now that does not mean you don't have to do your physical part in your healing, but the energy of your healing has to match the level of your faith.

I'm going to share more about the energy centers in the body called "chakras" as we proceed, but I wanted to first say that you can do anything when you can forgive. In addition, you have to know how to forgive to reap the rewards.

Forgiveness is an energy too; it frees you from past hurts and elevates your consciousness. If you want to be healed—mentally, physically, emotionally, and spiritually—you are going to have to forgive EVERYONE in your life that needs it!

The power of forgiveness continues long after you've forgiven someone. It's not an event, but an evolution. It transforms your perception of the past and prepares new neural pathways that minimize the feeling from that past hurt, and it does this all in the present moment. That's why when you repeat a story over and over again, it has a different emotional signature, and the more you have grown, the fainter the memory and the less painful the story becomes. That is why people like Elizabeth Smart can become advocates from their pain because they have now turned that pain into power.

The power of a "yes" energy means that when you allow yourself to forgive, not only yourself but the offender, you are giving yourself the greater power and raising your energy. Therefore, it doesn't matter if the person you forgive knows it or is present for it.

There are many simple techniques to raise your consciousness, and I will teach you these at the end of this chapter. You will be surprised how simple it is for you to create the Law of Attraction in your life.

Let's start with the breath—the most powerful energy of life and the most misused and misunderstood. Most people just breathe, but to have deliberate creations manifest in your life, you have to learn and master the energy centers for creation. For example, did you know there are several techniques for deliberate breathing?

Consciousness and energy create the nature of your reality.
~ Ramtha

The three primary types of breathing are:

1. **Eupnea breathing:** a mode of breathing that occurs at rest and does not require the cognitive thought of the individual.

2. **Diaphragmatic breathing**: a mode of breathing that requires the diaphragm to contract. For illustration purposes, check out this demonstration on YouTube https://www.YouTube.com/watch?v=Mg2ar-7_HfA.

3. **Costal breathing:** a mode of breathing that requires contraction of the intercostal muscles. For illustration purposes, check out this demonstration on YouTube https://www.YouTube.com/watch?v=lh-nkOmhS3A.

Energy flows where your attention goes!

With these three primary breathing techniques, you can learn how to move energy through your body. For example, meditation lowers the breathing and slows the heart rate as dancing heightens the breathing and raises the heart rate.

Friction is the movement of energy. Think of yourself as a magnet. Holding onto positive thoughts of what you want is how you attract them to you. Holding onto negative thoughts does the exact the same thing—it draws negative thoughts back to you. By moving energy in your body, you can change the way you think, feel, and act through a desire to release and let your past go, a devotion to returning to love, and discipline to do and become better.

Your body is the temple of the Holy Spirit, and the Holy Spirit is always communicating with you; however, you need to be vibrating at the frequency of higher-level consciousness. The Holy Spirit can't infiltrate your thinking when you are vibrating at low levels of energy; the ego does that.

So, how do you raise your frequency? There are several energy bands within your auric field, and when you are in harmony and balance, they create what we call "miracles" in your life.

There is no order of difficulty in miracles.
~ A Course in Miracles

These bands move around your body in a circular spiral. When in harmony, all is well. When you are angry or upset, this causes a disruption in the flow of energy.

There are seven primary chakras. Six of the chakras are in the body, and the seventh is located in the auric field (Crown Chakra).

The following explanation on chakras was taken from an article written by Maya Mendoza from zenlama.com. For more information and a deeper understanding of the chakras and how they work, I believe this website has the best explanation and practices for your higher learning (https://www.zenlama.com/the-7-chakras-a-beginners-guide-to-your-energy-system).

"THE 7 CHAKRAS — A BEGINNER'S GUIDE TO YOUR ENERGY SYSTEM

What on earth is a *chakra*, and what does it have to do with forgiveness? In many spiritual and healing disciplines and in the world of complementary medicine, the word chakra pops up often. That's fine if you know its meaning, but it can be confusing if you don't. Here's our simple summary of the seven chakras that covers what a chakra is and what the chakra system is all about.

The seven chakras are the energy centers in your body in which energy flows through. The word "chakra" is derived from the Sanskrit word meaning "wheel." Literally translated from the Hindi, it means "wheel of spinning energy." A chakra is like a whirling, vortex-like powerhouse of energy. Within our bodies, you have seven of these major energy centers and many more minor ones. Deepak Chopra says that each of the seven chakras are governed by spiritual laws or principles of consciousness that we can use to cultivate greater harmony, happiness, and wellbeing in our lives and in the world.

You can think of chakras as invisible, rechargeable batteries. They are charged and recharged through contact with the stream of cosmic energy in the atmosphere in much the same way that your home connects to a central power source within a city—the only difference is that this cosmic energy source is free.

Imagine a vertical power current similar to a fluorescent tube that runs from the top of the head to the base of the spine. Think of this as your primary source of energy. The seven major chakras are in the center of the body and are aligned with this vertical "power line."

Chakras connect your spiritual body to your physical one.

Chakras regulate the flow of energy throughout the electrical network (meridians) that runs through the physical body. The body's electrical system resembles the wiring in a house. It allows electrical current to be sent to every part, and it is ready for use when needed.

Sometimes chakras become blocked because of stress and emotional or physical problems. If the body's "energy system" cannot flow freely, it is likely that problems will occur. Irregular energy flow may cause physical illness and discomfort, or a sense of being mentally and emotionally out of balance.

This image shows where the main chakras are located in your body. You can read a brief, yet full, explanation for each chakra below."

"CHAKRA 7 — THE CROWN

Its color is **violet,** and it is located at the top of your head. It is associated with the cerebral cortex, central nervous system, and the pituitary gland. It is concerned with information, understanding, acceptance, and bliss. It is said to be your own place of connection to God—the chakra of divine purpose and personal destiny. Blockage can manifest as psychological problems."

"CHAKRA 6 — THE THIRD EYE (BROW CHAKRA)

Its color is **indigo** (a combination of red and blue). It is located at the center of your forehead, at eye level or slightly above. This chakra is used to question the spiritual nature of your life. It is the chakra of question, perception, and knowing. It is concerned with inner vision, intuition, and wisdom. Your dreams for this life and recollections of other lifetimes are held in this chakra. Blockage may manifest as problems like lack of foresight, mental rigidity, select-ive memory, and depression."

"CHAKRA 5. THE THROAT

Its color is **blue** or turquoise, and it is located within the throat. It is the chakra of communication, creativity, self-expression, and judgement. It is associated with your neck, shoulders, arms, hands, and your thyroid and parathyroid glands. It is concerned with the senses of inner and outer hearing, the synthesizing of ideas, healing, transformation, and purification. Blockage can show up as creative blocks, dishonesty, or general problems in communicating one's needs to others."

"CHAKRA 4 — THE HEART

Its color is **green,** and it is located within your heart. It is the center of love, compassion, harmony, and peace. The Asians say that this is the house of the soul. This chakra is associated with your lungs, heart, arms, hands, and thymus gland. We fall in love through our heart chakra, and then that feeling of unconditional love moves to the emotional center commonly known as the solar plexus.

After that, it moves into the sexual center, or base chakra, where powerful feelings of attraction can be released. When these energies move into the base chakra, we may have the desire to marry and settle down. Blockage can show itself as immune system weakness, lung and heart problems, or manifest as inhumanity, lack of compassion, or unprincipled behavior."

"CHAKRA 3 — THE SOLAR PLEXUS

Its color is **yellow,** and it is located a few inches above the navel in the solar plexus area. This chakra is concerned with your digestive system, muscles, pancreas, and adrenals. It is the seat of your emotional life. Feelings of personal power, laughter, joy, and anger are associated with this center. Your sensitivity, ambition, and ability to achieve are stored here. Blockage may manifest as anger, frustration, lack of direction, or a sense of victimization."

"Chakra 2 — The Sacral (Navel Chakra)

Its color is **orange,** and it is located between the base of your spine and your navel. It is associated with your lower abdomen, kidneys, bladder, circulatory system, and your reproductive organs and glands. It is concerned with emotion. This chakra represents desire, pleasure, sexuality, procreation, and creativity. Blockage may manifest as emotional problems, compulsive or obsessive behavior, and sexual guilt."

"Chakra 1 - The Base (Root Chakra)

Its color is **red,** and it is located at the perineum or base of your spine. It is the chakra closest to the earth. Its function is concerned with earthly grounding and physical survival. This chakra is associated with your legs, feet, bones, large intestines, and adrenal glands. It controls your fight-or-flight response. Blockage may manifest as paranoia, fear, procrastination, and defensiveness."

Now that you have a better understanding of how the energy centers work in your body, you can learn how to make them work in concert with the Law of Attraction.

Your spirit, mind, and body need to be in harmony and balance to manifest the desires of your heart. If there is a disturbance in your force, you may still manifest what you want; however, it may be more difficult for you to hold on to it. That can be a problem for some, but if the energy of your desire is powerful enough, you can jump any hurdle that may come your way.

It is also important to note that energy flows where your attention goes. The best way to determine if your chakras are out of balance is by the disease that shows up. For example, you might feel sluggish or disconnected or experience joint pain or back aches. If you are catching colds or sinus infections or find you have excess mucus, those are all indications that your chakras are out of balance. How do you realign? Get plenty of *rest, release* the need to control, and *rejuvenate* the body by reducing stress. Try turning off your devices for part of the day and sitting in silence. Or do as I do and put on some music and dance!

Reviving the body is essential to good mental health. Your mind and body need a break. The Bible says that God rested on the seventh day, not because He was tired, but because He wanted to emphasize the importance of caring for our bodies.

If you are tired and out of sorts, you lose your sense of clarity, become angry quickly, and can't make rational decisions.

FINALLY

WHAT I KNOW FOR SURE!

Forgiveness has been my life's work, and I learn something new every day on how to find forgiveness in the things I do and with the people I meet. My greatest lessons come from me. All the highs and lows of my life have made me a better me. I know that I have said and done things I regret, but I also know without these lessons I wouldn't be the person I am and for this I am grateful.

It costs you nothing to forgive. In fact, finding forgiveness in yourself will enable you to find the courage to forgive others. The benefit forgiveness gives you far exceeds the liabilities. Holding onto unresolved past hurts is like carrying the negative weight of the world around your neck. It doesn't help you, and it hurts everyone else. My grandmother used to say, "Who died and left you in charge?" That means you don't have the right to judge anyone until you are willing to judge yourself.

I've learned every moment is a choice between fear and love. You have a choice to release and let go or to hold on and suffer. Once you recognize that forgiveness makes you powerful, not weak, you will feel the true power of God.

Organizing your thinking is the gift you give yourself. Learn how to ask God for what you want and how to accept the gifts He gives to you. You don't have to understand the why of God; trust His power in your life. *A Course in Miracles* says, "If you cannot hear the Voice of God, it is because you do not choose to listen." Give up the need to be right and embrace the art of being happy.

I release and let go of anything that does not bring me joy. The moment something or someone attempts to rob me of my peace and happiness, I stop and ask myself what benefit they are bringing to my life. You must learn that you can't share big dreams with small-minded people. You have the power to remove those people from your life—even if they are family. Release and let go the need to fix others and focus on fixing yourself. Yes, it is true you can't divorce your family, but you can eliminate the amount of information you share with them.

Stop telling people your business! If you feel the need to share, then share with those who encourage you and the life you are creating. Misery loves company. You will discover that everyone doesn't believe in you the way you should believe in yourself.

Get clear about what matters most to you and hold that vision close to your heart. Release and let go of the naysayers; they don't want the highest and best for you. Like crabs in a barrel, they need for you to stay in the barrel with them. You don't have to act like you are better than them, because you aren't. You are unique!

Embrace your uniqueness and don't take on other people's stuff. Doing so only compromises the purpose God has sent you here to fulfill. Love people where they are and celebrate their individualities. When their goals and visions work in concert with yours, embrace them, but when they oppose yours, then move on. It is not your responsibility to change anyone; your job is to love them right where they are.

I have friends that I don't share things with. It doesn't mean I don't love them; it means I can't share everything with them. The Bible says, "When I was a child, I talked like a child, I thought like a child, I reasoned like a child. When I became an adult, I put the ways of childhood behind me" (1Cor. 13:11 NIV). It doesn't matter what others say. What matters is what you do with what they say. My parents lived their lives the way they wanted to, and my friends are living their lives the way they want to, so why shouldn't I live the life I want to?

No matter how big or small, joy is your birthright, and nothing should keep you from that space. You deserve to be happy and at peace, but only you can give yourself that. Don't be fooled by the illusions of your ego telling you anything different. God is and should be the only constant in your life. If you're not feeling the love of God, remember to do the five-finger exercise—middle finger, flick it and throw it away. It's that simple!

By releasing and letting go, you become more and more aware of the things you have, where you are, and the unlimited possibilities of a loving and prosperous future. The universe wants to give you your best life, and as *A Course in Miracles* says, "When your forgiveness is complete, you will have total gratitude, for you will see that everything has earned the right to love by being loving, even as your Self."

Be grateful for all the lessons you have learned; those lessons have made you who you are. Every struggle you have been through has enabled you to build the spiritual strength you need to be about your Father's business. The caterpillar had to fight to become a butterfly, and it had to fight and struggle all by itself. There is a butterfly inside of you yearning to share its beauty with the world.

Be grateful that you have the power to forgive. Appreciate that your heart is so full of God's love that you can only see the good in yourself and others. Like Mother Teresa said, "Lord, make me a channel of your peace, and where there is wrong, may I bring the spirit of forgiveness."

Listen to the Spirit of the living God within you; God will not abandon or forsake you. When something goes awry and you can't figure out why, be still and ask God to show you the lesson you need to learn from the situation. *Look, listen, and learn!* The Bible says, "If any of you lacks wisdom, let him ask God, who gives generously to all without reproach, and it will be given him" (James 1:5 ESV)

After you ask God for wisdom, wait on His answer! Instead of feeling sorry for yourself, just wait in expectation of the revelation He is bringing. Who knows, maybe this is happening to you to bring something good into your life even though your circumstances may seem bleak. Maybe things need to be shaken up in order for you to see what is ahead for you. Maybe God had to jack you up in order for you to move in the direction He wants you to go. There is a reason things happen, and you will continue to do the same things repeatedly until you understand the reason. God will always have your back, but the question is, do you have His back? Do you say you believe in God but question His motives for you? You can't be wishy-washy with God; you are all in or not!

Meditation will answer all those questions. Remember, listen and obey even if you don't understand! The answers are all around you, and God will show up in the most amazing ways. He will bring you answers from people, places, things, times, and events. Listen, pay attention, and KNOW the answers will come. Don't quit five minutes before your miracle shows up, and when those doubts and fears creep up, turn to that spiritual toolkit that keeps you in alignment with God. Don't be too proud to ask God for help; He is always available to you.

Don't just be grateful; value the littles things in life. Give thanks for being present to receive God's gifts. COVID-19 has affected all of us, so if you are healthy, have food to eat, and a place to sleep, then you should thank God every minute of every day. Energize those values and gifts and share them with others without condition. Get up, get out, and get moving in the direction of your dreams. Be the light you want to see in the world.

Yes, these are troublesome times, but they are not impossible times. Be creative and learn something new; there are a wealth of opportunities just waiting for you to seize. You are the change God has been waiting for, and with clarity, focus, ease, and grace, you can make a difference in your life and this world. Fear not and take the leap; there are miracles happening all around you, and God wants you to cash in on them all. God will respond to your song. Place your order with the universe and watch what God will do for you.

Live a life of deliberate creation—you can start with nothing, and out of nothing God will make a way for you. As Genie said to Aladdin, "Your wish is my command!" You get what you expect. Don't focus on who you were. Instead, focus on who you are. Bless the sins of your past; thank them for the lessons you've learned and move on.

The TV series *Greenleaf* is one of my favorite shows, and I have learned so many incredible life lessons from it. If you haven't seen the final episode, I highly suggest you watch it. After the death of Bishop Greenleaf, Lady Mae is asked to do a testament to his life and legacy. As she stands before the congregation, she starts her tribute by saying she has asked the Bishop what she should say. He has instructed her to *tell them something new*. She refers to Isaiah 43:18,19 (MSG), "Forget about what's happened; don't keep going over old history. Be alert, be present. I'm about to do something brand-new. It's bursting out! Don't you see it? There it is!"

She suggests we dream about the new—a new that has never been seen. She talks about the early days of Jesus' ministry—how He spoke in small places and in the homes of His new followers. Who would have heard of this "new thing?" No one! And there were multitudes of people who didn't believe what this carpenter from Nazareth was talking about because it was too radical for them to embrace.

Lady Mae then says, "My arms, heart, and mind are open. Dear God, make me NEW! Show me forgiveness where there can be none. Show me redemption when it is far too late. Show me acceptance where there is hate. And show me what I can't explain. Help us love our past enough to let it go and move forward into the future, I ask you, dear Jesus. MAKE ME NEW!"

Jesus asked His followers to forgive those who persecuted them. WHAT? Forgive those who had enslaved, raped, tortured, robbed, and separated them from their families? What in the world could He be asking these people to do? Love their enemies? Those folks must have thought He had been drinking too much wine. This was something new!

Forgive them? Love them? "Be kind to one another, tenderhearted, forgiving one another, as God in Christ forgave you" (Eph. 4:32 ESV). This is the *good news*. Don't forget that we receive forgiveness, and we should also be kind and forgiving to those around us. "Forgive as the Lord forgave you" (Col. 3:13 NIV). This was the *good news*, but it wasn't what they wanted to hear. They wanted to discuss how to defeat their oppressors, not love and forgive them. They were not interested in forgiving; they wanted to be freed from bondage, and they wanted Him to show them how to do that! So, how did Jesus finally get through to them? Through His deeds, He showed them. He hung out with the displaced and the disenfranchised, he healed the sick, and fed the hungry. He forgave Mary Magdalene and told her to go and sin no more. He challenged those who wanted to stone her by asking them to cast the first stone if they were free of sin. He did all of these NEW things. If you believe in Jesus, believe in that!

If you need help with forgiveness, you only have to remember one thing. You are here for God and for God only! Imagine what this world would be like if we made this our life's purpose. Do for your neighbor what you would do for God. If God can forgive all your transgressions, who are you not to forgive the transgressions of others? Your mission in this life is to fulfill the promise God placed on your heart. You don't serve man or woman; you serve God, and no one should distract you from that. Yes, it is easy to say and may be hard to do; however, it is worth making this your battle cry!

I have been blessed to live as long as I have, and I have learned many lessons along the way. What I know for sure is forgiveness is the key to having love in your life. You don't have time to hold grievances; God has work for you to do. Start your day talking to God and not watching the morning news, and God will be in charge of everything you do.

It's a new dawn, it's a new day,
it's a new life for me and I'm feeling good!

I hope that these words have been an inspiration to you, and if nothing else, you know God wants the highest and best for you. It takes work, dedication, and commitment, but it is yours for the asking.

FORGIVE-

For more information about my work, go to
www.DrCharletteManning.com and receive your free copy of
21 Steps to Living Your Best Life Now.

NOTES

Made in the USA
Middletown, DE
30 June 2021

43403196R00062